Software Testing Tips
Experiences & Realities

-Barış Sarıalioğlu-

COLOPHON

Title:	Software Testing Tips – Experiences & Realities
Author:	Barış Sarıalioğlu
Design & Layout:	Sera Seren

ISBN: 978-605-64140-2-2

To my wife, Simel...

For your love and caring,
Peace and compassion, support and patience.
For reviewing everything that I wrote (including e-mails!)
and for coming into my life,

Being my life...

CONTENTS

ACKNOWLEDGMENTS

I would like to thank to *everyone* around me for making this book real. Thanks for the inspiration, thanks for your trust, thanks for the invaluable experiences, and thanks for the things that you have taught me.

The most beautiful thing in testing is that you can feel its existence every night and day; and all the experiences of our everyday lives are replete with instances of it.

ABOUT THE BOOK

As software testers have always been under pressure due to poor-quality deliveries and project delays, I feel myself responsible for writing a practical book highlighting the realities and sharing my experiences. By this means, I will hopefully "depressurize" these innocent people.

Since ever-advancing technology in software development has triggered the evolution of computer applications, end products are becoming more complex day by day, with newly added features and increasing numbers of platforms available for reaching more and more customers.

In today's world, end users have a number of questions on their minds: what application should they use, what platform should they choose, which company will be the most secure and reliable? And this list grows drastically. Generally speaking, by the basic reason of economic apprehensions—the tendency to buy the fastest and most reliable products for the least amount of money—customers are deeply selective in their choices.

As a consequence, companies are working on delivering higher-quality products because they are aware of the fact that any kind of deficiency in these applications carries the risk of losing customer trust and may cause serious reputational damage. This inherently raises the level of "quality" objectives everywhere. For any software-producing company, basic prerequisites to be successful in delivering good software depend on having talented people and setting smart processes.

Throughout the book, I will be emphasizing a commonsense approach to software testing and trying to underline the key facts and their consequences. The advice contained in each respective section may remind you of some important things you might have missed and unwittingly neglected.

Hopefully you will find that all (or at least some!) of the observations in this book are very practical and applicable to your organization.

Have fun...

TIP 1
FINDING DEFECTS EARLY

All we know is that defects found early are easier and cheaper to fix than those found later, so let's focus on realizing early defect detection.

Anonymous

Testing is more than testing (and should start before testing).

Dorothy Graham

FINDING DEFECTS EARLY

I want to begin with this very well-known subject, because I deeply believe that it is the main driver of any quality assurance activity. Being a tester in the field for more than ten years has taught me that defects can be detected at any time, but the consequences solidly differ with respect to timing.

If you capture a very high-priority defect just before going live, people may hate you; but if you do it in the very initial days of the test execution, you become a hero. I think this is a very practical scenario that can be seen in any software project and it simply shows the importance of early defect detection.

Yes, it is clear that defects are generally and maybe "naturally" being found during the test phases (I mean the dynamic testing), but we should be aware of the fact that it is far better to detect them in earlier phases. Especially if static testing (reviews, walkthroughs, audits, and inspections) is properly executed, you can expect to have at least five to ten times more test effectiveness. If you do crowd testing this ratio becomes even greater, not lesser.

On the other hand, we need to remember that some defects can only be detected during system testing. But believe me, this ratio is not more than 50 percent. In other words, one can detect nearly half of the defects in earlier stages (analysis and coding) by realizing effective static testing approaches.

Note: This article is based on traditional (sequential) software development models such as Waterfall and V-Model.

TIP 2
YOU SHOULD STOP TESTING AT SOME POINT

Why do we never have time to do it right, but always have time to do it over?

Anonymous

YOU SHOULD STOP TESTING AT SOME POINT

As a famous saying goes, "There is always an end to everything beautiful." Unfortunately, this may also be applied to software testing. This is to say, you need to stop testing at some point, and this point should be a place like limbo: neither will you be completely risk-free (or bug-free) nor will you have lots of major bugs lying in the code undetected. In testing, we call this point "testing equilibrium."

Companies generally underestimate this fact, so we observe under- or over-testing scenarios. Upper managers generally think that over-testing is a very safe and logical solution if they have no budget and/or time constraints; on the other hand, they act deeply ungenerous when they have limited time and money. In that case they directly ask you to stop testing even very early. Often upper managers do not have a clear idea about what should be done for quality assurance, and so, unfortunately, the only things that count are budget and time.

I understand that project risks (e.g., budget limitations, staffing problems, time-to-market requirements, supplier issues) are critical drivers for making decisions about testing, but I also believe that product risks should be taken into consideration with other priorities of equal or at least similar weight.

On these slippery slopes, as a test manager or tester you need to be wise and organized. You should always remember to use risk-based testing approaches or at least prioritize and weight your test scenarios. This will definitely give you flexibility in making the best use of your staff and resources to lower the risks and help you to do adequate contingency planning and estimation for test-related risks to be done.

Once risk assessment and monitoring is realized, you can identify your "testing equilibrium."

TIP 3
TESTING SHOULD NOT ONLY SHOW DEFECTS

The principal objective of software testing is to give confidence in the software.

P. D. Coward

TESTING SHOULD NOT ONLY SHOW DEFECTS

As testers we always feel the pressure of defect detection, and we are expected to find as many as we can. And we must ensure that all these defects are fixed, which is always a painful struggle. In any software development project, the percentage of failed and passed test cases are main drivers for quality approvals and for "go"/"no go" decisions.

When upper managers or project leaders observe a test result report consisting of 90 percent failures, they naturally become upset. And all the project team, especially the developers, feel even worse. I know that rehabilitating the project team is not the testers' responsibility, but we should be fair and objective in our feedback, without any doubts. If we observe 90 percent failure rate in any test execution report, we need to look at the mirror and ask ourselves: "Am I developing very complex test cases?" And the answer should be definitely: "No!"

Of course, we cannot say that the only reason for failures is test case complexity. Sometimes very simple test cases may fail, and with similar logic, very complex test cases may pass. These can both happen due to the quality characteristics of any analysis, design, or development product.

We cannot reach a conclusion on the result of any test execution activity before we run the test cases. They may all fail in some context and may all pass in some other. However, in my experience I believe that the most benefit and learning can be captured by reaching 30 to 70 percent probability of failures.

In other words, if nearly half of the test cases are failing, then we can be quite sure that our test cases are prepared in proper complexity, our test suite results in less redundant/repetitive work, and our defects are more unique (fewer duplicate defects). Furthermore, we can be quite sure about the functioning features as well as the nonfunctioning ones.

As I have mentioned above, testers should be very careful about the test execution results. We need to find defects and show the deficiencies; concurrently, we should be motivating and showing our confidence in the product or in the project. At the end of the day, we are in the same boat, and all of us will be responsible for the good and the bad.

Believe me: it is impossible to have a 100 percent nonfunctioning system after hundreds of fully staffed days of software development. Some things should be definitely working, and you should recognize them as well!

TIP 4
BUG-FREE CODE NEVER HAPPENS

The only certainties in life are death, taxes, and bugs in code.

Anonymous

Failure is not an option. It comes bundled with the software.

Anonymous

BUG-FREE CODE NEVER HAPPENS

Having indicated our confidence in any code, now it is time to acknowledge the other side of the coin: the "bug-free code never happens" dilemma. Yes, we know that some developers are heroes, some applications are very simple to code, and some technologies are very well adapted, but still we can be sure that each and every kind of software development activity will raise bugs. If you want to have bug-free applications then you need to stop coding at all. This seems to be the only logical solution!

Once we examine the major root causes of defects, we shall once more see that bug-free code will never happen. Let's go through some root causes: Missing Requirements, Incomplete Analysis, Configuration Errors, Violation of Usability Criteria, Violation of Regulations, Coding Errors, Platform/Service Deficiencies, and the list continually grows. Ultimately, with all these complexities and dependencies, one cannot talk about any bug-free code.

Sometimes developers say, "It works on my machine!" or, "This bug is not because of our code, it is because of someone else's!" In all these conditions, the main responsibility of a tester is to keep calm and try to be persuasive. Never forget that all developers tend to reject defects. This is a genetic algorithm and cannot be changed at a stroke.

From another perspective, if you want to assess a test team's performance and motivation, you can have a look at the defects they found (count, content, and quality). Generally speaking, if you observe defect-free test execution, it means that the team has some deficiencies. Maybe they are lacking in domain know-how, maybe they do not have sufficient QA skills, or maybe the developers are too conservative in welcoming defects. But you cannot ever conclude that the code quality is very high and this is the reason for the defect scarcity. You have my word on this!

There are several software development methodologies you can follow to help keep code close to bug-free. For instance, in test-driven development (TDD), all the code is written to pass certain predefined test cases. If you exercise TDD in a structured manner, then you may have fewer defects.

Any type of software development model cannot guarantee you will have zero defects; however, some models can give better results once they are properly matched with the project objectives and the relevant context.

TIP 5
ANYONE CAN BE A TESTER! IS IT TRUE?

f u cn rd ths, u cn gt a gd jb n sftwr tstng.

Anonymous

ANYONE CAN BE A TESTER! IS IT TRUE?

No, it is not true! Despite what many non-testers think, software testing is a deep and complex activity. When you think of it as pressing a button and waiting for the response, surely you will miss a lot of things: its importance in any software development life cycle, its place of bridging the gap between developers and business analysts, its higher-level perspective of seeing the whole picture, its frameworks, its standards, its maturity levels, its regulatory necessity, its tools, its techniques, and some hundreds of other logical and valuable grounds.

In contrast to the above, most people tend to think that testing is a job that anyone can perform. In other words, they think that anyone can be a tester! These ideas are funny from a certain perspective, but they illustrate the real big bias against being a tester as well.

Yes, almost all computer engineering/science graduates have the goal of being developers rather than becoming testers, but research and my individual experiences taught me that the requirements of these two roles (developer and tester) are more or less the same. You should be strong in both technical and soft skills. You should be good at QA skills, scripting, coding, databases, and computer networks, and you should also have business domain know-how, negotiating skills, problem-solving capacity, and analytical thinking ability.

In my experience, I have never eye witnessed a tester being treated badly (at least, no one has ever tried poisoning one!). They have same rights, same appearances, same reputation, same salaries and same promotion opportunities.

- Do you still have no desire to be a tester?
- OK, then, you can continue with what you are doing! ☺

TIP 6
TESTERS CAN (!) STOP BAD SOFTWARE

If you don't care about quality, you can meet any other requirement.

Gerald M. Weinberg

TESTERS CAN (!) STOP BAD SOFTWARE

Regrettably, this is not the case in real life. Yes, it is true that testers want to have the rejection power in our hands, but under tight deadlines and upper management pressures quite a lot of the deliveries happen with a bunch of deficiencies and unfixed defects.

Maybe you are asking, how can this even happen? Let me assure you, this is a very standard daily life scene in any software project. Everyone in the project knows that the software will crash, but no one can prevent it. That's all because of the unrealistic delivery promises given to business by IT upper managers. If these people cannot stand against relentless business demands, how could a test manager or a tester do so? It is sad but true.

Unfortunately, the very first thing that I learned from my early software testing experiences is that finishing the task on time is always more important than doing it in a proper way. In other words, you are expected to finish testing on time rather than do it with high quality and coverage.

From another perspective, when developers realize that the "promised delivery" will happen whether or not the test department says OK, then how can we expect high quality and accuracy from them? Yes, developers will try to fix the high-priority bugs, but will their respect for testers remain the same? Will there be any accountability between the developers and testers?

Without doubt, if you want to have a bug-free application running in production, you should give authority to your testers and empower your test teams. If they can reject bad software or even stop a delivery, you will see that unit tests will be more popular among development teams, defect turnaround time will drastically reduce, and developers will become more agile and responsive.

Since better software requires not only better development but also better analysis, better design, and better testing, this rejection power smoothly increases the competition between project members (testers, developers, and business analysts), and you will even observe improvements in analysis documents and design artifacts.

The bottom line is that quality will definitely improve. Worth a try, isn't it?

TIP 7
SEGREGATION OF DUTIES: INDEPENDENT TESTERS

We have as many testers as we have developers. And testers spend all their time testing, and developers spend half their time testing. We're more of a testing, a quality software organization than we're a software organization.

Bill Gates

Muddied responsibilities create unwanted risk.

Kevin Coleman

SEGREGATION OF DUTIES: INDEPENDENT TESTERS

Testers should be independent. Yes, you are reading it correctly: they should be unchained from any other IT divisions/departments like development, analysis, system, or infrastructure. In order to expect meaningful, rational, and, especially, "unbiased" testing, you need to make test departments free and keep them out of any irrelevant commitments.

I have experienced this several times. In one of the companies I worked for, I was executing tests and reporting to a software development director. At another company, I was positioned under an analysis manager. If you have an organizational structure like these, you will neither have controlling/auditing power nor independence.

Imagine you are reporting a development team's bugs and your boss, who was originally a developer, comes and asks you to "chill out" and give developers time and breathing space. Or another boss asks you to discontinue some quality reporting (because it hurts!) and another time asks you to publish some "nonsense" quality metrics in favor of some departments, divisions, or projects. All of these are not so pleasant experiences. Especially if you are measuring quality, you should not be someone's man.

Luckily, in some sectors government entities exist that control and regulate QA issues. They set rules and audit companies in order to check if the regulations are followed and the related IT governance frameworks are deployed. With this external power, the dream of having independent testers and test organizations becomes more and more real.

Beyond any doubt, whether you establish independent testing yourself or someone does it for you, it will bring many benefits. Some of the most critical ones include:

- Unbiased testing
- Standardization of test processes, deliverables, and outputs
- Reduction in test efforts
- Increasing responsibilities, consequently improving quality
- Better user acceptance testing (UAT) and improved customer satisfaction
- Accelerated software development life cycles (SDLCs)
- And many others as well...

Now is the time for you to break the chains and free your testers!

TIP 8
MEASURE YOUR TESTING

*Anything can be made measurable in some way,
which is superior to not measuring it at all.*

Tom Gilb

MEASURE YOUR TESTING

I was always a numbers guy, who goes in for showing everything with quantities and referencing outcomes to objective measures. In private life, it is sometimes hard and sometimes very easy. In order to show my love and dedication to my wife, I always remind her with numbers. Sometimes these can be the dates of our anniversaries and sometimes they can be the number of days we haven't seen each other.

In testing, these measurements are easier to extract and present. When you are doing any unmeasured or unquantifiable testing activity, you need to be very careful. Without any metrics and measures, software testing becomes a meaningless and unreal activity. Imagine, in any project, that you are not aware of the total effort you have expended and total number of defects you have found. Under these circumstances, how can you identify the weakest points and bottlenecks?

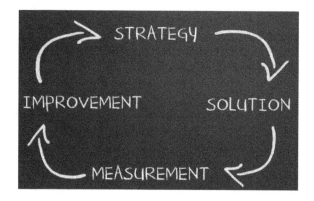

I always remember and respect the famous saying: "If you want to improve something, you need to measure it first." And I truly believe this. If you want to show the bad as well as the good, you need to measure your testing and present quantifiable results. In general, logical and clever managers require numerical evidence; they are not satisfied with any nonnumeric information.

Let me list some of the favorite test metrics that I love to capture and display. I believe some of them should be very easy for you to get, and for the rest you may try your chances. They are:

- Total Test Effort and Test Efficiency (including schedule and cost variances)
- Test Execution Metrics (# of Pass, Fail, Block, Inconclusive test cases)
- Test Effectiveness (# of defects found in system test / total # of defects found in all phases)
- Total # of Defects, Priorities, Severities, Root Causes (system test, regression, UAT, and live)
- Defect Turnaround Time (time required for developers to fix defects)
- Defect Rejection Ratio (ratio of false/invalid defects)
- Defect Reopen Ratio (ratio of unfixed/failing "ready to test" defects)
- Defect Density (per development day or line of code) and Defect Detection Ratio (per day or per testing effort)
- Test Coverage, Requirement Coverage, Requirements Stability, and some others you may like more...

If you collect and analyze the above metrics accurately, you will be several steps ahead of others who don't.

TIP 9
DO NOT EVER OVERLAP SYSTEM TESTING AND UAT

Quality is the ally of schedule and cost, not their adversary. If we have to sacrifice quality to meet schedule, it's because we are doing the job wrong from the very beginning.

James A. Ward

DO NOT EVER OVERLAP SYSTEM TESTING AND UAT

Under tight project deadlines, one of the favorite and most misapplied actions is to overlap test phases—in other words, doing system testing simultaneously with user acceptance testing. Yes, it may sound very schedule-friendly and logical, if you regard these activities as if they are independent. But unfortunately, in software testing they are closely correlated.

In a project, milestones and schedules are directly derived from the "critical path." As we all may encounter, critical path, according to Project Management Institute (PMI), is the "longest sequence of activities in a project plan which must be completed on time for the project to complete on the due date." And also, "an activity on the critical path cannot be started until its predecessor activity is complete." As system and user acceptance testing phases are succeeding activities, you can neither merge them nor do them in parallel.

I am sure some of you are doing this and asking why you should not. It is because, if you do them in parallel, you will have an immature and buggy system in front of your users, you will have lots of duplicated bugs coming from testers and business users, your defect turnaround time will increase drastically (developers will slow down), and the control over test environments and releases will be weakened (especially if you are using separate environments for system testing and UAT).

Moreover, you will be faced with monitoring problems, user/customer trust issues, and several other complicated outcomes.

Ultimately, you will never finish your testing on time (100 percent tested), and you will never realize any advantage by starting UAT earlier than the right time.

If you are committed to short-run promises and have a "save the day" approach, then you can feel the joy and pride of starting UAT early and making your customers temporarily happy (definitely for a short time!). But you should always keep in mind that earlier "small" delays are always less sorrowful than, and are preferable to, late "big" ones.

The choice is yours.

> ***Note:*** *In some iterative and/or modular approaches (e.g., agile development), you can overlap test phases of different modules, sprints, or deliveries. You may have experienced the benefits. In this chapter, I am rather talking about traditional software development models such as Waterfall and V-Model.*

TIP 10
TESTERS ARE GENERALLY NOT ANYONE'S FAVORITE PEOPLE

Software testers succeed where others fail.

Anonymous

TESTERS ARE GENERALLY NOT ANYONE'S FAVORITE PEOPLE

It is true. Testers are not amongst the favorite people in any IT organization. It is not only because they are defect finders but also because of the misperception in peoples' minds that "Being a tester is not a good thing, so testers cannot be good people!" Sounds logical...

Through my entire career, I have lived with this phenomenon. There is always a bias against you; developers do not like you, managers generally find you repellant, and employers think that you are underachieving. Despite this, you try to do your job, execute your tests, find bugs, communicate with developers, and convince people, yet in the final days you must stand against criticism, time pressure, and poor quality.

Test releases never happen on time, unit tests are never completed, all other activities except testing consume more effort than estimated—but *you* need to be accurate, timely, clear, precise, and punctual. In short, you need to and should consume less time than estimated!

After all, you are not the favorite person. This is a tester's destiny.

Although aware that the aforementioned experiences cannot be reversed in a split second, I nevertheless seek to champion testers at all times. You can join me by taking some initial steps and changing your thinking about the following usual misconceptions:

- Anybody can do testing; it is not a big deal.
- Testers are happy when a project fails.
- Testers do not know anything about coding, scripting, databases, and computer networks.
- Testers are always pessimistic.
- Testing is very boring and repetitive.
- Testers cannot be promoted, testers cannot be entrepreneurs, testers cannot be senior managers.

The entire list above is untrue. Let me highlight the correct ones below;

- Anybody can do testing; but it differs a lot when you consider the outcomes.
- Testers are happy when they find bugs, just because they feel themselves useful. On the bottom line, testers want the projects they work on to succeed as much as anyone.
- Testers are encouraged to have skills on coding, scripting, databases, and computer networks. Technical testers are on the rise.
- Testers are naturally pessimistic and this brings optimism to the projects.
- Testing can be really exciting and interesting. It can differ a lot depending on your perspective and appreciation.
- Testers can promote, testers can be entrepreneurs and testers can be senior managers.

Tried and trusted…

TIP 11
DESTRUCTIVE TESTERS VS. CONSTRUCTIVE DEVELOPERS

Folk wisdom and natural belief:
Testers are destructors, developers are constructors.

However, during runtime, things may reverse;
good testing is "undisputedly" constructive and bad
coding is "sure as death" destructive.

Anonymous

DESTRUCTIVE TESTERS VS. CONSTRUCTIVE DEVELOPERS

I assure you that testers are suspicious people, unquestionably. As a result, they are perceived as negative and pessimistic. In some cases, people also find them destructive. These are all typical and natural consequences of this bloody business of testing. If you are unfortunate enough to decide on a testing career, you need to prepare yourself beforehand. You need to break down the prejudices; you need to do something.

Everything started with the first bug ever detected in history. Thus far, everyone believed that bugs are pretty and small creatures and they have their rights to live within the spaces reserved for them by their originators! If this can be considered as true, then I accept I am a destructive, negative, and pessimistic person. But if not, then I will ask you to think twice.

Meanwhile, it will be helpful to know that testers are generally not satisfied, they are always curious, they cannot be persuaded easily, they never trust you 100 percent, they push you to fix things, they report you to upper management, they escalate the unresolved issues, they announce bad quality, they stand against releases, they try to teach you things that you already knew, and do some other annoying things as well. If you ask me why, I will tell you that it is all because testers are defenders of high quality.

Rather than being a "bad" constructive developer, I would prefer to be a "good" destructive tester. If you are really good at what you are doing, you will be "constructive" beyond any doubts. Am I right?

TIP 12
NO PAIN, NO GAIN: OUTSOURCING

If you deprive yourself of outsourcing and your competitors do not, you're putting yourself out of business.

Lee Kuan Yew

NO PAIN, NO GAIN: OUTSOURCING

Nowadays, test outsourcing occurs all too often. Yes, from many perspectives it is logical and beneficial to outsource testing, but you need to be careful about setting your expectations and doing your homework.

First, you need to have a delivery model and a well-defined methodology. If you do not have enough experience and processes to deliver your test activities, you will definitely fail the first day. I have experienced test divisions trying to outsource some of their activities but which lacked test deliverables, functional/requirement documents, and experienced staff. If you do not have at least some of these, do not dream about outsourcing!

Second, you need to be patient about the outcomes. If you expect too much in the very beginning, then you will be disappointed. All outsourcing models require some time to deliver satisfactory results. Before reaching the break-even point, you should not expect so many benefits. It will be like a swimmer diving deep into the water and hitting the ground. You need to experience the bottom to rise higher. Before hitting the ground, you will be overcoming learning, adaptation, transition, and handover; and while you are rising, you will be having the joy of reliability, flexibility, cost savings, operational expertise, and speed to market. Worth it!

Third, you need to focus on organizational issues. If you outsource onsite, you need to be careful about co-location, collaboration, and motivation of the entire team (including in-house staff). You should be careful about forming your teams; you should treat your outsource staff fairly and consider their problems as much as you do those of your in-house employees. If anyone in the group ever senses a distinction between permanent employees and outsource staff, then problems will rise. This is a sensitive issue.

Apart from the above, another major ingredient for success in any test outsourcing operation is establishing effective service level management. In response to your organization's needs, you have to set up your goals and require your vendors to operate under a variety of service level agreements (SLAs). Any outsourcing solution that is built upon an SLA-based delivery model is much more efficient and controllable than body shopping alternatives.

Experienced, tested, and approved!

TIP 13
PLEASE ESTIMATE "RATIONAL" TEST EFFORTS

Projects that set out to achieve "aggressive" schedules probably take longer to complete than they would have if they have started with more reasonable schedules.

Tom DeMarco

PLEASE ESTIMATE "RATIONAL" TEST EFFORTS

"No budget left for testing! Unfortunately, we need to ask you to stop/finish before the predetermined milestone."

This is a very common and practical way of cutting any testing budget. Yes, the example is a little vague and harsh, but it's very common. With all my experience and knowledge, I am against any kind of testing budget reductions, because they are nothing but quality reducers. I have seen many projects with aggressive schedules, but they never finished on time. Why is that?

It is all because the effort estimations are generally biased and unrealistic. Project managers believe that giving unrealistic (early, aggressive) milestones will get them promoted, but it won't. The only thing they get is a bitter taste in their mouths after postponing the final delivery a number of times. I accept that I am a little bit pessimistic here, but this is what I have been observing for years, independent of industry, technology, and people.

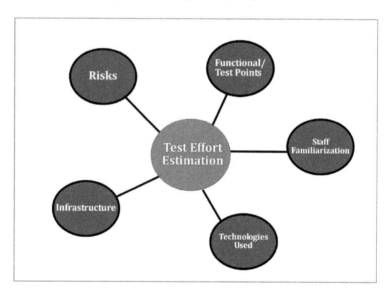

Another misleading practice is estimating testing effort as a percentage of development time. Believers of this approach first estimate their development efforts and then decide on a relative testing effort that fits! I'd argue that testing effort is much more closely correlated to other variables than to development time. This approach can be deceptive and relativistic. Be careful!

No one can be sure that 100 units of development effort requires 90 units of testing effort or 110 units of testing effort or even 1,000 units of testing effort without basing the estimates on consistent foundations. These estimations are variable with respect to application complexity, code complexity, document quality, network speed, QA staff skills, familiarization, domain know-how, test types, team sizes, software development methodology, benchmark values of previous projects, and many other factors.

I will not be explaining how to estimate real testing efforts here (Google does it so well), but you can use many of the proven methodologies such as test point analysis, functional point analysis, task-based estimation, requirement-based estimation, scenario-based estimation, three-point analysis, Delphi technique, work breakdown structure (WBS), and so on.

Take it from me, these are definitely better and more realistic ways of estimating your testing efforts. As testing is nothing but a tradeoff between time, budget, and quality, you should first specify your position on these three phenomena, and then you can even estimate your testing efforts with your gut feeling. (Of course, if time or budget is more important for you than quality...)

TIP 14
BUY TOOLS IF YOU NEED THEM

A fool with a tool is still a fool.

Grady Booch

BUY TOOLS IF YOU NEED THEM

A big problem in any organization, and a very easy way of squandering money, is buying software that will never be used.

I feel a need to write about this subject because I have seen millions of dollars of investments that were thrown away on software that remained untouched or utilized only minimally. Maybe this seems unreasonable to you at first glance, but I assure you that many organizations are keen on buying software without considering the necessity and return. They just buy the software for the sake of telling people, "Yes, we have the necessary software for this activity."

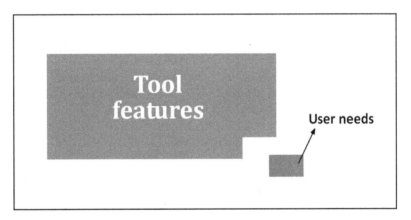

When we narrow the subject to software testing, everything is more or less the same. Organizations invest heavily in buying any kind of testing software, but they generally don't care or know enough about their utilization. I remember having three test management tools at the same time and still using Excel sheets for writing and maintaining the test cases. What a waste!

Vendors, on the other hand, know very well how to attract people. They prepare perfect presentations about their products, create virtual environments for making proof of concepts (PoCs), and try to make you feel comfortable and impressed. Surely this comfort and optimistic ambiance lasts until just after the tools are purchased!

You generally notice major deficiencies and observe issues related to your own environment (internal network, firewall, operating system, servers, and so on) just after you intend to use them. But why?

Everything was really perfect in the PoC, what has happened?

The answer is very straightforward: you relied on a simple virtual experience and did not try the tool in your own environment. That's it! Below are tips for an effective PoC; I think all are known but not strictly followed.

- Clarify your needs and requirements
- Try to experience as many tools as possible—one tool per issue is never enough
- Try the tools in your own environment (network, firewall, OS, DBs, applications, etc.)
- Check the integration between tools (e.g., Test Management Tool and Defect Tracking Tool)
- Be careful about buying bundle products merely because bundles seem to be cheaper options; most of the time they boost the amount of shelfware in your organization
- Check the maintenance costs—a tool can be cheap for buying but can also be expensive for maintaining
- Check open-source alternatives and complements—you don't have to pay for everything
- Do not buy more licenses than needed—be a little bit of a skinflint
- Be patient about the return; you need to commit and sacrifice for the perfect utilization—things never happen by themselves
- Do not buy many tools at a time; take your time and proceed step by step—remember, accuracy and perfection require dedication

There are many others that can be added to the above list, yet one last thing I want to say is that if you don't really need a tool for realizing any software testing activity, then stay away from the tool (e.g., be ad hoc or toolless). Buying a fancy tool will never make you go one step further unless you need it. Instead it may result in the opposite by bringing inefficiencies and cost overruns.

TIP 15
EARLY INVOLVEMENT: IS IT A DREAM?

If you don't have information or expertise early, there is a good possibility that parts of the design will have to be reworked at a later stage. Redoing the design will impact cost, schedule, and possibly quality.

Kris Buys

EARLY INVOLVEMENT: IS IT A DREAM?

Testers are absolutely absent in early project activities. Why is that? I really don't know the main reason, but I feel that people value testing as a late life-cycle activity (which is 100 percent wrong) and they underestimate testers' necessity and contribution for activities such as project planning, requirement analysis, risk management, effort/budget estimation, product design, coding, and also static testing.

When testers are excluded from all these activities, they become unaware of the critical project foundations of budget, schedule, risks, and design. As a result they get weaker and lose their flexibility and determination. On the other hand, project stakeholders remain unaware of testers' point of view and their valuable insight in assessing project risks, estimating test efforts, and analyzing requirements. Under these circumstances, no one can speak about collaborative and transparent work.

Besides, involving testers too late in the project results in the continuation of defects that could have been resolved early in the project; in later stages they become much more expensive to solve. If project budget is everyone's responsibility, then early involvement of testers should also be.

When we dive a little bit deeper, we can see many more obstacles. Just after the test planning and preparation starts, unless testers are involved early in the project, they spend a lot of their time on just understanding the aim and scope of the project, observing the risky areas and realizing the defective parts. Without this intelligence they naturally struggle to produce something valuable, and, as a result, test efficiency and effectiveness significantly drops.

Given this, I urge you to get your testers involved in projects early on—even if you feel that it is already too late. Whichever phases your projects are in, starting testing at the earliest possible time is still important. Trust me on this!

Testers: Never think that it is too late; do your best to get involved early. Otherwise you have to be responsible for low quality, regardless of being the very last and most neglected person on the project team.

TIP 16
DO NOT "AUTOMATE" TO SHOW OFF

Answer the question and then proceed:
Is this really going to be worth it?

Anonymous

DO NOT "AUTOMATE" TO SHOW OFF

Why do people like showing off? Because they want to impress other people or at least feel comfortable with themselves.

So many subjects in software testing can appear to be complicated, but none as much as test automation. Almost everyone (including me) has an opinion about it, and none (including mine) can be taken as a general truth. Then what am I supposed to say here?

Let me share my perspective: if you don't need automation, don't waste your time, and instead continue on with what you are doing. You don't need to automate your test cases just to prove that you are a smart tester or you are a member of a competent test team.

Generally, this entire dilemma starts with the misperception that automation is always faster than manual testing. This idea is generally triggered and spread by inexperienced/biased testers or upper managers (we like them anyway). My response is a big "No!" Don't leap to that conclusion. It depends on many variables, like test development efforts, test maintenance efforts, technologies/tools that are used, frequency/prevalence of your test execution, complexity of test environments, and test automation familiarization.

If you have concluded that test automation is what you need, then you have to consider its scope and volume. To what extent do you need to automate your test cases? How many of them should be automated?

Since software testing can continue on infinitely, you can automate test cases forever. But as time goes by, you will see that most of these test cases become obsolete. So you need to decide on the scope and volume of test automation by checking your team size, staff availability, and necessity. And we know that maintenance of these automated cases are still done by humans (most of the time), so we should take that into consideration.

There are some test activities that should not be automated at all: for example, penetration tests (a kind of security test). I cannot imagine a device that behaves exactly like a hacker and intelligently tries to attack any information system. Not possible, not logical.

What about user acceptance testing (UAT)? I believe it will not fit at all. User interaction is and should be included in any UAT process, so there is no point to automating user acceptance test cases. Likewise, in exploratory and usability testing, I see no grounds for automation. Because these tests are being executed for capturing real experiences and outcomes, automation will only make them unreal rather than making them efficient and faster.

All in all, test automation is not a short-term exercise or even a quick decision. If you want to experience its benefits, you need to be patient and keep being rational and consistent. I know some people are on the side of "everything can be automatable," but here we are questioning whether it would be worth the effort to do that automation.

TIP 17
AUTOMATION WILL NEVER REPLACE HUMAN TESTING

There are certain things that automation is good at and certain things humans are good at and it seems to me a hybrid approach is better. What I want is automation that makes my job as a human easier. Automation is good at analyzing data and noticing patterns. It is not good at determining relevance and making judgment calls. Fortunately humans excel at judgment.

James Whittaker

AUTOMATION WILL NEVER REPLACE HUMAN TESTING

This is every testers' concern: "Will automation replace me?" Let me say, "No, not in the near future." But, anyway, you still have a chance to be beaten by a computer. It depends what industry you are in and what activities you are executing.

Although I stand for the "anything can be automated in some way" approach, I still credit the argument that there should be someone (probably a human) to test the results of automation or at least update/maintain the environment. So full computer invasion should still be beyond our imagination—at least my imagination!

Some testing activities require real human touch, validation, judgment, and interaction. Human users still are accepting the products rather than computers. Consequently, test automation will be meaningful to some extent, and the rest will be done by humans.

In particular, the operational/routine test activities such as data entry, data preparation, static GUI checks, product installations, periodic regression tests, network transactions/messaging, logging, and monitoring issues can be automated to make things easier for testers. So test automation seems to be a good idea for simplifying our workload, not for replacing us with computers.

On the other hand, some organizations still have very high test automation percentages, like 90 percent or even almost 100 percent. But do you know why? It is because they cannot survive without automation. Since technology and infrastructure are main drivers for automation decisions, sometimes they won't allow you to do things manually. For instance, if your test execution requires thousands of network messages/transactions/requests to be sent or processed in a very limited time, test automation will become inevitable.

"I'm the only human that works here. The other 17,000 employees are computerized robots. Would you like to speak with C76-78X?"

If you follow an iterative development approach like test-driven development (TDD), then you can have high automation ratios with unit-level test cases. This is because your processes and way of implementing solutions give you no room/space for manual testing.

All in all, we are all safe. At least humans are needed for realizing test automation to replace themselves!

TIP 18
AUTOMATION IS NOT FOR BUG DETECTION

Finding bugs is a great objective for testing—but it is not a good objective for automation.

Dorothy Graham

AUTOMATION IS NOT FOR BUG DETECTION

Yes, all the test activities are done with the aim of finding defects; however, the perception should be different for "test automation." Let me consult a dictionary first. Cambridge Online Dictionary says *automation* means "to make a process in a factory or office operate by machines or computers, in order to reduce the amount of work done by humans and the time taken to do the work." So, by a logical interpretation, test automation should be an activity done to consume less effort and create operational efficiency.

As a result, we should not see test automation as responsible for catching defects. Rather, we should blame it for not reducing our testing efforts or bringing any efficiency to our operational manual testing activities. Automation itself does not consist of any special intelligent logic to detect bugs, as is the case with manual testing. It is a combination of written procedures and technology used for imitating real user behavior (as much as it can), and that's why it is not fair to position automation as your bug detector.

From a different viewpoint, test automation is much more efficient when it is used for regression testing. In other words, automation gives you returns when the test cases are executed frequently and when the system under test is stable/mature (so you spend less time on maintenance efforts). Within any regression testing, I am more focused on 100 percent pass ratios (presenting high quality) rather than catching a lot of defects and problems (presenting low quality). Yes, I want to find major bugs as well, but the first priority is always having a clean run without problems.

There is a small nuance here.

When you analyze any automated regression test suite with an aim of detecting as many bugs as you can, you are *not* on the right track. But if you judge any regression test suite with the thought of expecting zero defects and nothing but a very few major/critical bugs, you are on the way!

From my point of view, automated test cases are used more for showing that a system is working properly, and the manual ones are for showing a system's flaws. As I am a defender of the concept that testing is not just for bug detection but also for showing our confidence, I believe we can achieve an equilibrium between automation and manual testing.

After all, balance is the key to life, isn't it?

TIP 19
USABILITY TESTING: WORTH THE INVESTMENT

It is far better to adapt the technology to the user than to force the user to adapt to the technology.

Larry Marine

USABILITY TESTING: WORTH THE INVESTMENT

A very recent trend in the software industry, and a very subjective issue to be solved, is usability. Despite being in testing for more than ten years, I had never participated in a complete usability testing session before 2012. Maybe I was a little bit late to recognize the use of usability testing; but as I always say, "It is better late than never."

I always felt that testing was quite a structured activity that heavily relied on quantitative (in other words, "objective") grounds, but after I experienced things like usability and usability testing, I changed my mind. Yes, sometimes testing can be deeply subjective, and its results can also be varied and dependent. It is hard to accept, but it is correct. Especially for a person like me, who has always been binary (0s or 1s, yes or no) all his life, it is interesting that some technical problems or issues may have several results.

The activity of capturing user behavior and measuring their satisfaction on any software product is really equitable and inclusive. Until usability testing, users were only "accepting" the product rather than "liking" it. But with usability testing, now is their time to criticize the software and complain about it when their special needs are not fulfilled. Users are rising!

When I dive deeply into usability testing, I see how big this framework is and how it might go further. There are lots of techniques and technology behind it and all are absolutely adding value to the user experience and usability arguments. I remember utilizing a tool that could record and measure user activity and setting up a usability testing area in one of my former jobs. Even though we were quite new to the area of usability testing, we were able to manage the process of collecting any kind of user interaction data and making sense of the outcomes.

After some time, we were mature enough to do our own usability testing. We did video capturing, retrospective think-aloud, logging and timing, and we specified our personas. We then collected and gave meaning to the data, like time on task, number of errors, mouse mileage, mouse clicks count, and survey/questionnaire results. When you add all these pieces together, you climb the maturity levels of user experience.

If you are working in a B2C company that has never conducted any usability activity and are using web and mobile apps as distribution channels, you can try to take some small steps, as we did before. Any kind of measurement realized on your user segments will give you insight on what you are doing and how satisfied your customers/users are.

Having professional assistance surely is a way to handle the issues of user experience and usability, but giving a try to build something yourself will be more valuable for warming up. Whether you invest in a professional service or you try to execute it your way, usability testing is worth every penny.

Let me finish by listing some insights from several valuable resources and experiences:

- More than 50 percent of software development time is consumed by usability-related deficiencies.
- More than 60 percent of customers/users are not so happy with the applications they use and think that they are neglected.
- Usability testing with a couple of testers will give you flexibility in addressing the majority of the usability

problems; remember the 80–20 rule!

- Any investment in usability testing will pay back up to a hundred times.
- Include generation C (connected, communicating, content-centric, computerized, community-oriented, always clicking) in your usability testing plans. Remember, apps are more extensively used by people who are extremely digitally native and technology oriented.

I hope that I have convinced you to do usability testing now. You can immediately start doing questionnaire-based usability testing by handing out SUMI (Software Usability Measurement Inventory) questionnaires to your users/customers. Free versions are available everywhere. Just customize one for yourself and take the initial step!

TIP 20
BE FLEXIBLE IN HIRING JUNIOR TESTERS

Because a thing seems difficult for you, do not think it impossible for anyone to accomplish.

Marcus Aurelius

BE FLEXIBLE IN HIRING JUNIOR TESTERS

I spend a couple of hours on the Internet searching job ads for junior testers, and again I am disappointed by "our" search for perfection. I am surprised with the requirements we (employers and managers) attach to this position and the way we search for fresh candidates.

Now I can really understand why we are lacking sufficient numbers of applications and why our job ads are staying open forever. The answer is clear: we expect too much from a junior tester, and we will never find an appropriate candidate who is really super qualified and technology native! We are not aware that job ads that are full of requirements and lots of technical expectations are repellent rather than attractive.

Yes, people are searching for valuable jobs and challenging environments, but they are not looking for any interview experiences in which they will be humiliated and belittled. They are not interested in finding out how underqualified they are; especially when they examine themselves against a job ad.

Let me show you my thinking. Below is a very typical Junior Tester job ad. Let's look if we have similar feelings or not:

→ BS or MS in computer, electrical/electronics, or industrial engineering.

- Why not statistics, mathematics, civil engineering, or even architecture? Is it necessary to be an engineer of some area related to computers? In my experience, the answer is "No." I have known very qualified testers coming from business administration, finance, and even from painting!

→ Minimum 2 years of experience in software test environment, preferably involving writing test procedures, designing test cases, manual or automated test execution.

- No "junior" tester can have experience, am I right?

→ Knowledge of database technologies and SQL is a must.

- To initiate several SQL inquiries and prepare test data, no junior tester need be proficient in database technologies! They can learn it in a couple of weeks...

→ Knowledge of Unix/Linux is a must.

- No, it is not. You can learn the basics in couple of days!

→ Experience using testing tools (preferably X, Y, and Z).

- They don't teach how to use testing tools in universities. We need to teach them to junior testers rather than expecting them to know.

→ X, Y, and Z certifications in software testing will be a plus.

- Yes, it will be a plus, but you cannot expect a new graduate or a junior tester to have these certifications. Certifications are generally needed for becoming seniors, not juniors!

→ Outstanding interpersonal and communication skills.

- Can be revised as "good" instead of "outstanding." Remember, no one is perfect and perfect is the enemy of good!

→ Good command of written and spoken English.

- Yes, knowing English is important (at least it is necessary for reading this book), but it should not be mandatory. If you are doing local business and the context (or content) is not English at all, you may hire non-English-speaking junior testers. Believe me, they can do what you want!

→ Available to work flexible hours.
  • What do you mean by flexible?

→ Male candidates should have no military obligations or postponed for at least two years. (Can be the case in countries where military service is mandatory.)
  • All junior males have military obligations!

"First job interview?"

I want to conclude by saying that we are hiring humans, not machines. As recruiters, if we do not show our flexibility, how can we expect it from others? With all the requirements and written procedures, we only lose our flexibility and eliminate our chances to find proper candidates.

If we are looking for junior testers, it is better to look for creativity, analytical thinking, communication skills, and enthusiasm rather than database skills, Linux know-how, software testing experience, and certifications.

Do not forget: "Commitment matters, qualification doesn't."

TIP 21
APPLY DISTRIBUTED LEADERSHIP

You cannot be a leader, and ask other people to follow you, unless you know how to follow, too.

Sam Rayburn

APPLY DISTRIBUTED LEADERSHIP

I am lucky that I was involved in Professor Deborah Ancona's class at MIT Sloan, where she taught us distributed leadership and its benefits. With all my experience, I am a full supporter of the idea of spreading leadership functions over organizations for cultivating the knowledge and practice of managing and leading.

What about the correlation between distributed leadership and software testing?

I think these two issues are strongly coupled. In any test organization or activity, leaders and executers are always necessary. In any issue about software testing, there exists a nontechnical governing side. Sometimes you do planning, sometimes you do scheduling, sometimes you guide people, sometimes you control deadlines, sometimes you report results, and the list grows.

I have seen many advantages of "distributed leadership" through my entire career as a tester. If people lead each other and roles are collectively distributed, I observe people developing more rapidly. Besides, you create a more fair and participative environment. In such organizations, testers become more responsible, confident, and respectful to each other.

You can never build up the same environment in one-man organizations. A single person collects all the leadership responsibilities, and the rest become just executers. I advise these traditional and "heroic" people to at least follow and spread the principle that a tester should be his or her own leader.

From another perspective, distributed leadership gives you the power of using your time efficiently and allows you to be more productive. Imagine you are a test manager doing administrative tasks all day. (I remember the old days!) After a point, you will turn into an operational maintenance officer. No innovation, no technology, no execution, and especially no TESTING. What a dull life!

If you want to use the advantage of a variety of perspectives, you should also distribute your leadership activities. We all know that dedication and employee satisfaction is essential in any organization. If this organization is a test organization, satisfaction is even more critical. If you want to make your testers feel that they are contributing to the success of your company, you need to distribute leadership. Never forget, being a powerful leader requires much more than just technical skills and knowledge.

If you still want to be the only leader, leastways I am asking you to lead your staff in such a way as to make them lead themselves. It should be as easy as pie; what do you think?

TIP 22
DO RANDOM CHECKING

Routine is the enemy of creativity and innovation.

Anonymous

DO RANDOM CHECKING

What do I mean by random checking? Let me give the Cambridge Online Dictionary definition first: "a check on items taken from a group without any special selection." And the meaning of randomization is: "to make something random [so that it happens or is chosen by chance], especially as a way of making a test fairer or more accurate." Now it makes sense. If randomization can make a test fairer or more accurate, then we need to use it, am I right?

To my way of thinking, random checking also gives you flexibility to be spontaneous and mysterious. Yes, in testing you need to be spontaneous and also mysterious sometimes. Imagine a group of testers reporting to you, and just because of the time you spent with them you become less selective and more permissive during your daily routine. If you are an approver of any test execution activity, the last thing you need is an invalid or an unreliable test result. In order to mitigate the risk of any failures, sometimes you need to be more interrogative.

I advise you to randomly check the results (or any output) and see whether they are precise and accurate. But each time you need to do this for different content (randomly selected) using a different approach (again, randomly selected). If your suspiciousness is sensed by the group, then you may be faced with confidence and loyalty problems. Besides, if your methods and areas of focus are predictable then the power of random checking diminishes, since the rest of the group will be aware of what you are going to check beforehand.

Anyhow, it is always good to know that someone is (or may be) randomly controlling your output and that if any inattention or failure is captured, you are in trouble. I don't mean to never trust people, but that keeping an eye on any output and double checking any result is far better than doing nothing but just showing your trust. Believe me, it is not as bad as it feels.

If these checks are never conducted at random but instead are conducted on any suspicious situation or failure, then there is a risk that you will face even bigger problems. Imagine some live system failures observed, and they are all because of your unreliable test activity. At times like these, you will be surely sorry for not having an external checking/controlling entity around you.

On the other hand, by randomly checking your teams, you are sweeping away the probability of any unfair situation for who gets checked and who doesn't. From this point of view, you will be sure that random checking that affects everyone also affects everyone equally.

Managers, paired testers, project leaders, and other related staff cannot afford to do random checking on everyone all the time. Occasional random checking will also reduce the burden on these people to do checking at other times, and allow them to focus on being effective at their primary jobs.

So, routinely break your routine, and do something unexpected and daring for the betterment of testing and testers.

TIP 23
PERFORMANCE TEST TOOLS NEED CALIBRATION

Unfortunately, performance test tools do not emulate the exact same behavior a real user would show when accessing any application. You need to calibrate them first to have accurate results.

Roland Van Leusden

PERFORMANCE TEST TOOLS NEED CALIBRATION

Frankly speaking, so far I haven't seen an organization engage in performance testing properly. Maybe I am a little bit unlucky or a little bit pessimistic (or even a little bit exaggerating), but this is the case! In some organizations we were using inappropriate tools, in some we were lacking deliverables, processes, and reporting, and in others we were lacking performance requirements.

But most importantly, for all of the above we were unaware of the performance tool calibration phenomenon. Putting it another way, we were 100 percent relying on the tools' behavior and output. Having realized this fact, I can easily say that processes, deliverables, reporting, requirements, and everything else you have successfully adapted in performance testing are worthless if you are neglecting tool calibration. I have told you; truth is bitter!

Do all these mean that the performance tests so far (at least the ones I have executed!) do not reflect real results (and can be discarded as trash)? No, I cannot say that; but I do have serious doubts. Hopefully, my ex-supervisors and managers won't read this book, or at least this page!

At Romania Testing Community Conference 2013, an interesting session was held by Roland Van Leusden, a colleague and a friend from the Netherlands, which explained this fact in perfect detail. I have great respect for Roland's research and know-how about the subject, so I asked him to give me some details about it. I am lucky that he didn't refuse my request. Here is what he had to say:

> "When we buy a ruler, we expect that it is correct within a certain tolerance. When we buy a more expensive ruler, it comes with a calibration certificate that states under which conditions the ruler will be exactly one meter long. With performance test tooling, there is no such calibration and certification; you just have to believe that when you run with fifty users it will behave and produce a load equal to fifty real users.
>
> After investigation I found that this is not the case when you use the tools with their default settings. You need to analyze what the user is doing at client, network, and server level with your application; this will be your reference. The good thing is that most tools can be adjusted to create similar behavior to the real user; it requires, however, in-depth knowledge of your application at the various levels and tooling. To get accurate, production-like results, you need to calibrate the tooling and validate the output, to make the right decisions for the best user experience."

Any objections?

TIP 24
HOW TO SELECT THE RIGHT TOOL

And the promise is that the deal is so good that we can't refuse.

The Godfather (1972)

HOW TO SELECT THE RIGHT TOOL

One of the most challenging issues is tool selection. No matter which kind of tool you are looking for, it is always a headache. Whether you have some budget or nothing, you still have to consider all the possible options and make the right decision at the end.

On the other hand, testing is a really interrelated issue. It covers and touches a lot of streams: project management, test management, defects management, requirements management, test automation, data management, performance testing, and many more.

In order to be effective in any of the test activities, you need to differentiate yourself through a depth of tool knowledge; and sometimes you need to be ready for playing a consultant role in the environment you work in. If you want to establish a sustainable and transparent environment, your initial goal should be selecting the right tool at the right time with the right associations.

For instance, if you want to get rid of Excel sheets (I like them, by the way) and replace them with a test management tool, it is not enough for you just to buy the test management tool. You need to consider the related processes (like defect tracking, release management, time management, etc.), roles, deliverables, and associations with requirements and other test basis deliverables. Consequently, a powerful tool with dozens of proven features cannot fulfill your requirements unless positioned correctly in the software delivery life cycle.

Functionality should not be the only criteria when selecting a tool. Many other things need to be considered. If you are willing, I want to give you some hints and tricks for selecting tools.

Sure, my ideas will be a little bit generic, but I believe that they will provide you insight. I have experienced tens of commercial and open-source tools in many industries (defense, telco, IT, finance), and I believe that experience is the best teacher.

I will be listing my priorities about four different tools: Test Management, Mobile App Test Automation, Defect Tracking, and Test Data Management. I hope the ideas will remind you of some criteria to consider while you are doing PoCs. Let me start.

Test Management Tool

- Check test artifacts, objects, and deliverables associated with the tool.
- Check if a customizable folder structure for test cases and scenarios is available.
- Check import and export functionalities for test artifacts (test plans, cases, scripts, scenarios).
- Check updating mechanism (e.g., bulk update).
- Check test artifact versioning (how the version history of any updated artifact is handled).
- Check test preconditions and exit criteria functionality.
- Check reusability and modularity.
- Check the search engine associated with the tool.
- Check test data insertion functionality (how test data can be inserted into a test case or step).
- Check ordering and scheduling functionalities for test cases and scripts.
- Check prioritization and weighting for test artifacts.
- Check association with requirements and defects.
- Check association with test automation tools.

- Check reporting capabilities (test coverage, pass, fail, blocked, not conclusive, number of defects, priorities, etc.).
- Check performance and scalability (especially if a considerable number of people will use the tool).

Mobile Test Automation Tool

- Check jail breaking and rooting.
- Check if manual scripting (hand-coding) is allowed and IDE/language is adoptable.
- Real device (recommended) or emulator support.
- Object and/or image recognition.
- Functionalities supported—swipe, drag and drop, zoom, scrolling, pinching, rotating, shaking, etc.
- Check integration with test management tools and/or test management capabilities.
- Check scheduling and ordering of test cases/scenarios.
- Check cross-platform support.
- Check reporting capabilities.
- Check database access and data connectors (white/gray box testing).

Defect Tracking Tool

- Check association with test management and test automation tools.
- Check defect workflow functionality and customization (to trace status as open, in-progress, works as designed, not reproducible, ready to test, and so on).
- Check reporting capabilities.
- Check notification features (to notify developers, testers, or any person about new defects, changed status, and resolved defects).
- Check integration with release management tools (to associate defects with releases).
- Check special attributes such as priority, severity, root cause, resolution date, defect description, module, version, found in (to have all the necessary attributes for a defect).
- Check import and export functionality (to have all defects in an Excel sheet).
- Check defect work item dashboards and their functionality

(to easily display defect attributes in any special filter condition).

- Check attachment functionality (to attach and use screen shots, logs, and traces).
- Check archiving functionality (to archive some project or application areas).
- Check dependency functionality (to link one defect to another).

Test Data Management Tool

- Check data subsetting and data masking functionalities.
- Check data compression rates.
- Check automatic discovery of database relations.
- Check performance and CPU/memory utilization.
- Check integration with test management tools and/or test management capabilities.
- Check scheduling/automation.
- Check supported database technologies.
- Check reporting and logging capabilities.
- Check privacy and security features.

And a final reminder about all the above: test and utilize the tool in your own environment (servers, network, firewall, applications, databases, etc.), because tools will never function as smoothly as they do in vendor presentations or virtual environments.

TIP 25
TOOL-DRIVEN PROCESSES VS. PROCESS-DRIVEN TOOLS

You Wear a Crown but You're No King

A song by Blessthefall

TOOL-DRIVEN PROCESSES VS. PROCESS-DRIVEN TOOLS

Now, please let me address the correct timing of selecting tools. All the aforementioned actions will surely assist you in selecting the right tool, provided you do all your selections at the right time.

Let me make it more clear by analyzing the dilemma: tool-driven processes vs. process-driven tools. I have sadly experienced many organizations (including the ones I worked for) selecting their tools before defining their processes. This is not a good approach, since you lose control over the tools by letting them design your processes and drive your daily operational activities. These are just tools; they are not your strategies, plans, or organizational goals, so don't let them take control. Instead, you make your tools help you in achieving your goals. This is feasible only with correct timing. Before setting a common language within your test department and defining your test processes (e.g., policies, strategies, basis, life cycle, deliverables, and so on), you should not talk about any tools or even PoCs.

Below is the pyramid of test governance. You can take it as a guideline for yourself and go up step by step. When you are finished with training, processes, organization, and techniques, the last building block shall be the tools.

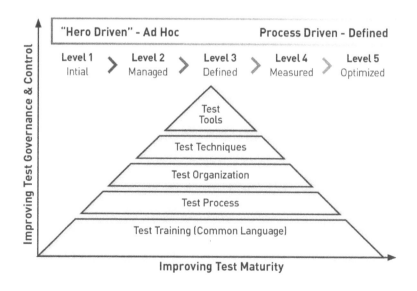

If you want to be the king and to wear the crown, you need to make sure that you are standing on solid ground and have a crown that will fit you.

Otherwise, the crown may fall off quickly—or you wear it but you become no king.

TIP 26
SET SMARTER GOALS

A goal properly set is halfway reached.

Zig Ziglar

SET SMARTER GOALS

Professional life is all about setting goals and trying to achieve them. When you achieve your goals, you become successful; when you fail, problems arise. In testing, we do the same. We have projects to finish, deadlines to follow, test cases to execute, and along the way we generally neglect the most important thing. We never question the goals that we have been assigned, and we generally fail to consider if these goals are smart or not.

Let me start by sharing one of my experiences. While I was working on a very big project years ago, one of the managers gave me a task to import all the project's test cases into a test management tool, and he said the task was urgent. I hated the task from the very start because I have never been interested in operational or purposeless activities. I was sure that the imported test cases would never be used again.

We were using Excel sheets for storing the test cases, and the importer tool at that time was not so advanced. Consequently, I spent about three weeks (at seventy-five hours a week) to complete this bloody task. First, I found all the test cases—they were not handed to me on the first day—then I converted them into meaningful artifacts for the old-fashioned importer, and then I imported them into the test management tool. Finally, I organized them in the tool database, and I was finished.

After I was finished, I sent an e-mail to the manager and said the task was completed. Three days later, I got a reply with two sentences: "Thanks, but you were a little bit late. I said the task was urgent but you delivered it in three weeks."

I read the e-mail about a hundred times and decided to reply him. Below is my reply:

"Thanks for your valuable feedback, but the task you assigned was not **specific** because it didn't involve any details and clear explanations.

"Also it was not **measurable** because the total number of test cases was not known in the very beginning.

81

"It was not **attainable** because you did not ask my opinion and we were not agreed about anything.

"It was not **relevant** because I have recently heard that a new test management tool was just purchased and will be in used in a couple of weeks. And the good news is the data in the old tool will not be transferable (cannot be migrated into the new tool database).

"And finally, it was not **time-bound** because you did not give me a deadline or a time limit to finish the task."

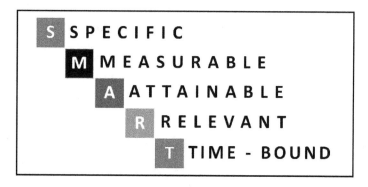

You may find me a little bit aggressive, but it was all correct. The "SMART criteria" helped me defend myself and assisted me in grasping the essence of setting smarter goals. From that day on, I have always followed this valuable framework. Whether I am a goal setter or a follower, I pay attention to be smart and realistic.

As testers, we always face challenging tasks and goals. Before getting too caught up in worrying about how to achieve these goals, first check them to determine if they are specific, measurable, attainable, relevant, and time-bound. These five characteristics are the things you need to hold on to when you are not sure about any consequences or outcome. They will definitely assist you in heading in the right direction.

Asking questions is a natural feature of testing, so never hesitate to question your goals. It is better to ask questions beforehand. Otherwise you may waste your time (like I did) and find yourself in a situation of explaining to people how you were successful but did not achieve the goals.

TIP 27
TESTING IN A CROSS-CULTURAL TEAM

Every man is in certain respects a) like every other man, b) like some other man, c) like no other man.

Kluckhohn & Murray

TESTING IN A CROSS-CULTURAL TEAM

Whether you are working in IT or any other industry, communicating with people of differing cultures is extremely difficult. To be honest, it is much more difficult than solving a complex test automation problem! It often requires a broad angle of thinking and understanding. When a conflict arises in a cross-cultural team, the operational activities become even more complex. Without deep analysis and digestion of how cultures interoperate and create problems, theoretical management approaches often make things worse.

I am not sure how I linked cross-cultural phenomena to software testing, but I think they should be somehow related. At least human beings are main actors for both, right?

In order to make this correlation stronger, I will share an experience about a cross-cultural incident that happened in the past in which I was playing the lead and will try to convince you that this is a subject worth deeper investigation.

The incident was regarding the performance appraisal of a test consultant in one of my previous companies. Just after her second month in the division, we had gone through the mandatory process of performance evaluation. The problem occurred in our face-to-face meeting, as she told me that she was not satisfied with the grade I had given to her.

She continued by explaining how she was not aware of the expectations, how she was not involved in her target/score card creation, and how the grading criteria was not individual but was corporate-wide. She added that she was also willing to evaluate me as her supervisor, and she wanted me to explain to her what kind of performance management courses I had completed so far!

After I got this shocking response, I tried to explain to her the details about the current performance measurement system and in a way tried to convince her about the current system's effectiveness and fairness. I also told her that we had no better option, and other firms are even worse. [I used a blend of two different rationalization techniques: "denial of responsibility" and "social weighting." No chance for you to find these in a software testing book!]

After we finished and she regained her temper, I felt deeply guilty about my speech. I defended our way of measuring performance without exactly analyzing its deficiencies. As an ethical and detail-oriented person (which I believe myself to be), I decided to make a thorough investigation of our performance measurement system, aiming to uncover deficiencies from both logical and ethical perspectives.

As I had never been faced with any complaints about the performance system from my local staff before, I had thought that everything was fine and we were on the right track. With some rational thinking, I found several striking root causes and major deficiencies.

Let me try to emphasize the underlying causes which brought me to the complex situation:

- The consultant came from a country where, as I have gleaned from articles/studies, people are extremely attentive to punctuality. They tend to get annoyed when the timing is not accurate and they are not informed prior to any kind of occasion. Consequently, a sudden/quick performance evaluation can be disruptive, as timing/organization/agenda is expected to be very clear and smooth.

- She was coming from a large power distance culture.

- Performance measures are very critical for them to express themselves, and they tend to look for explicitly defined criteria in terms of owner, unit of measure, collection frequency, data attributes, expected values (targets), and thresholds.

- As people of this culture are usually very diplomatic and fair, they easily become dissatisfied when their feedback is not collected and their opinions are not valued on any issue (in our case, feedback/contributions about the performance measurement criteria).

- The current performance management system was very dependent on project scores and corporate goals. Individual items were generally missing on the target card. As these people are individualists rather than collectivists, they would be more satisfied with individual performance evaluation items rather than corporate/generic ones.

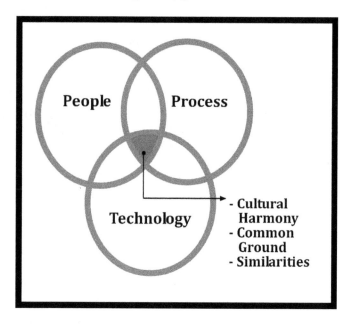

Unfortunately, these are not written in any software testing book, and if you do not pay attention to social matters as well as technical ones, you suffer a lot. My cross-cultural experiences taught me that! If you want to achieve a high organizational capability, you need to

understand the importance of
- Being aware of cross-cultural phenomenon (differences or misunderstandings)
- Taking responsibility for bridging the cultural gaps
- Training your staff on cultural differences
- Establishing both social and work-related activities for team members
- Developing more effective leadership by understanding the cultural dimensions of individualism vs. collectivism, masculinity vs. femininity, future orientation, power distance, and uncertainty avoidance

Hopefully this section will trigger you to focus on the root causes and consequences of some organizational incidents by helping you to develop a cross-cultural point of view.

Some problems require special mind-set and experience. Technology cannot solve all your problems!

TIP 28
WHAT EXPLORATORY TESTING IS NOT

Exploratory Testing is not so much a thing that you do; it's far more a way that you think.

Michael Bolton

WHAT EXPLORATORY TESTING IS NOT

It would be a pity if I did not write about exploratory testing in this book. Rather than explaining what exploratory testing *is*, I will try to explain what exploratory testing is *not*.

All people in the software testing industry are somehow, someway keen on doing exploratory testing. You could also say that all humans have exploratory skills as well.

I mean it. If you are doing a structured/scripted test activity and design your test cases with a very specific technique with predefined expected results, then it is better not to talk about exploratory testing. But if this is not the case, then you can say that you are more or less doing some kind of exploratory testing.

I encourage my staff and colleagues by telling them that testers are born to be exploratory people. If our job is to analyze a system and find its bugs, this contains exploration by its nature. And for everyone, exploration means something. Whether following an unnamed pattern or using an ad hoc technique, we should count it as exploratory testing.

What about documentation? Most people still think that if you are doing exploratory testing, you should not have any documents or any written procedures. This is not true!

Any exploratory testing activity can be documented and also can rely on some written test basis. It doesn't mean that you lose your exploration power by writing documents. Sometimes you do it for announcing test results, sometimes you do it for checking requirements, and sometimes you do it for learning something.

If you document your exploratory scenarios and repeat them in a future release, then I can say that you are not doing exploratory testing. Once repeated, exploratory testing becomes un-exploratory testing. This is another important characteristic.

Another misperception is about who should do exploratory testing. In contrast to the majority of software testing professionals, some specialists still think that this activity should only be done by people who don't have any domain/business know-how and/or even any testing skills. My answer again will be, "NO, this is not necessary."

Any testing professional and/or any business analyst with a solid domain know-how can surely do exploratory testing. Exploration itself does not have any borders or thresholds. So you cannot say that a non-IT person without any business know-how can do better exploratory testing than an IT professional with solid business skills. It is up to the context you are in and the personal characteristics, analytical thinking capability, and imagination you possess.

What about people who misprize exploratory testing? These people generally defend the idea of doing exploratory testing at the end of all other "valuable" and "structured" test activities. They think that exploratory testing is a "nice to have" activity, but don't want to spend so much time on this unstructured way of detecting bugs.

Again, I will take a stand against these ideas and say that exploratory testing is not an activity that can be done at the end of everything. If you have a vision of doing exploratory testing after completing all other activities, please do not waste your time with it. Instead, continue by doing other tests that you are keen on.

Finally, my last point will be about tools. Some people think that exploratory testing can only be done without tools! Fortunately, it can be done with tools. It is not mandatory to use a tool for it, but if you need to have a tool to record what you have done, to track the defects you have found, to monitor which resources you have used, to document the procedures you follow, or to report the results of your testing, please do so.

By the way, there also exist commercial and open-source tools just for doing exploratory testing!

To sum up:

- Every test activity has some exploration in it.
- Every tester has some exploratory skills.
- Exploratory tests can be done by anyone, including experts, business analysts, developers, users, and testers.
- Exploratory testing can make use of documents and can be documented.
- Exploratory testing can be done with or without tools.
- Once repeated, exploratory testing becomes un-exploratory testing.
- Exploratory testing is not a last-minute activity; it requires planning, effort, and dedication.

TIP 29
TOO BIG TO BE NEGLECTED: TEST DATA

In God we trust. All others must bring data.

W. Edwards Deming

TOO BIG TO BE NEGLECTED: TEST DATA

Since software testing is mostly a data-driven activity, and testers spend at least half of their efforts in managing the test data (creating, obtaining, using, storing, refreshing, masking, subsetting, and tracking), I want to write about this subject and try to give you some useful ideas and information.

Let me start by telling you a little bit about the "big data" phenomenon. Several investigations indicate that more than half of global companies are storing more than 100 terabytes (TB) of data. And these data are expected to double in the next two years' time. Apart from this, companies still find themselves immature about handling their data (which is quite correct), and almost all of them are willing to invest in this area for a better governance.

While companies are making the use of these information oceans and derive profits from the data they store, at the same time they suffer from it. It is obvious that no company can cope with data growth by just increasing their hardware capacity. Companies need to find smart solutions for this inevitable growth.

When we narrow the subject to testing, we observe that IT organizations are deeply focusing on the collection and organization of data for their testing processes. The ability to control this process and use test data has become the key competitive advantage for these organizations because benefits of such mechanisms will outweigh their disadvantages. Ultimately, test data management plays a vital role in any software development project. Unstructured processes may lead organizations to:

- Do inadequate testing (poor quality of product)
- Be unresponsive (increased time to market)
- Perform redundant operations and rework (increased costs)
- Be noncompliant with regulatory norms, especially on data confidentiality and usage

We all know that testing is a very critical part of good software development; nevertheless, test data management gets only minimal attention from us. Why is that? I really do not know.

Maybe it is because we are more focused on execution rather than preparation, or we are more focused on the result of the game rather than how we are playing. Whatever the root cause is, we need to accept that many test failures are caused by inconsistencies in the test data. Therefore, we need to be sure that we have constructed an efficient test data management process.

If we do so, then we can be quite certain that test metrics are not biased and we do not cause any interruptions and time loss through our test execution process. On the following page, I list the most essential activities and processes to achieve a complete test data management process. If you follow them in a structured manner, then you can talk about test efficiency, cost reduction, and acceleration. Here they are:

- Initiate a demand tracking process for managing the test data demands and their status
  - Including creation of the workflow and utilization of a activity tracking tool
- Include test data analysis activities in the test planning phase
  - Specify all the necessary data parameters, like depth (amount of data), breadth (variation of data), scope (relevancy of test data to the test objectives), sensitivity, and architecture (physical structure of the test data)
- Set and frequently measure your test data objectives
  - Reliability, accessibility, completeness, consistency, integrity, timeliness, security, and so on
- Include test data preparation activities in the project plan and test development phase
  - Estimate efforts for test data analysis and preparation
- Follow a step-by-step approach (below you can see the high-level picture)
  - Extracting (from the source database; you can do sub-setting if necessary)
  - Masking (for desensitizing the test data and ensuring that there exists no confidential customer information that is against any legislation or legal enforcement)
  - Loading (into the target database)

When we go even deeper, we shall observe that every different testing activity (e.g., test type or test level) requires different test data. The following chart hopefully will help you in determining what volume and variation of data you need while you are executing different levels and/or types of testing.

Type of Testing	Test Data Requirements	
	Volume (Depth)	Variation (Breadth)
Unit Testing	Small	Simple
Integration Testing	Small	Simple
Sanity/QA Check	Small-Medium	Simple
Exploratory Testing	Small-Medium	Wide
Smoke Testing	Small	Wide
System Testing	Medium	Simple
System Integration Testing	High	Wide
Regression Testing	Variable	Variable
User Acceptance	Medium-High	Production-like

To clarify your test data requirements, there are questions you should ask yourself, including:

- What kind of data is needed?
- How much data is needed?
- When is the data needed?
- Who will use the data?
- Where will it be extracted, and where will it be loaded?
- Does it have any dependencies?
- Is it sensitive, and how will the data be secured?
- How will the governance be done?
- How will the data be refreshed?

Once you have gathered all the answers and you are satisfied, then you can be sure that you are on the right track.

No matter which approach you choose to handle the challenges of the important subject of test data management, the basic requirements for you to be successful are a combination of good test cases and test data along with the proper usage of tools to help you automate extraction, transformation, and governance of the data being used.

If you want to see results, you need to play well in the game. You either will have excuses or results; the choice is yours...

TIP 30
NEGATIVE TESTING CAN BE REALLY POSITIVE

Negative testing can not only find significant failures, but can produce invaluable strategic information about the risk model underlying testing, and allow overall confidence in the quality of the system.

James Lyndsay

NEGATIVE TESTING CAN BE REALLY POSITIVE

Let me tell you first what negative testing means to me. It can be any kind of test execution activity based on improper or inconvenient scenarios. It may show a system is properly working or not—so it is not different from any other test activity from this perspective—but the type of actions taken by the tester are negatively driven.

I observe some misinterpretations of the definition of negative testing. Surely, I respect every opinion, but the negativeness of this test activity is not coming from the aim of showing that some system is not functioning, rather it is coming from the way we approach the system. In this case, testers are negative, not the systems. They are basically entering invalid inputs or executing some unexpected user behavior.

Hopefully, we are on common ground now. (If not, you can still read my ideas. At least they prove that your ideas are better!)

Let me move on to the next topic. People say that testers are pessimistic by nature, but their scenarios are by default positive! How can this happen?

The answer is clear: it is all because of the test basis. To be more precise, we naturally observe requirements, analysis deliverables, business process diagrams, and functional documents all written and prepared in positive manners. It sounds logical, because we do not expect directly negative expressions in requirements. In other words, requirements generally tell us what a system will do rather than what it won't do.

As a consequence, test scenarios tend to be positive from the nature of the basis on which we wrote them. What, then, can we do?

In my work environment, I encourage people to write at least 20–25 percent of their test cases negatively. To be honest, I don't like such arbitrary numbers but feel that this is necessary in order to ensure that sufficient attention is given to negative testing.

Let me relate an experience I had:

In a very complex transformation project, we were about to finish functional testing. Lots of bugs were found and fixed, and some modules seemed to be mature enough for user acceptance tests (UATs). Just before we officially announced the UAT phase, some colleagues told me that they had found many defects while they were trying some unwritten negative test scenarios.

Until that moment, we were neither concentrating on nor encouraging any negative testing activity. Just after that, I did some research into negative testing, and at first, I was not thrilled. I said to myself, this cannot be that effective.

When I returned to the office, I asked the guys to show me their work. They showed me some negative scenarios, like entering five characters into a field where it should be a minimum of eight, typing letters in numeric fields, concurrently logging into the system from several different browsers and checking the systems authentication/authorization behavior, checking data limitations and attachment size controls, and so many other invalid actions.

Frankly speaking, all the test cases failed! It was really impressive to see such intense negativity in a single run, but the things I saw completely changed my mind. From that moment on, I was a fan of negative testing.

And if you wonder what happened to the project, it was postponed for three months...

SOME PEOPLE ANSWERING THE QUESTION
"WHAT IS TESTING?"

"Testing is what my husband does. It pays for our mortgage and buys me beautiful gifts. Apart from that, it is a process of measurement. If we are talking about a product, testing is measurement of the conformity in its design."

Simel Sarıalioğlu, my wife (Lawyer)

"Trying to evaluate the relative correctness of anything."

Yeşim Sarıalioğlu, my mom (Chemical Engineer)

"Testing is assessing the trustworthiness."

Başak Altan, my sister (Banker)

"Perfecting efforts to those who are not willing to pay fluffy maintenance bills for their systems."

Emre Can Doğruyol, friend (Finance Specialist)

"Testing is the art of revealing the truth. Facts can be so painful that, due to a small bug, software may crash. Think of it as a software in a plane, which means it may **even** fall with all the passengers."

Ahmet Duran, friend (Software Developer/Architect)

"Testing reminds me of a process of controlling devices to check if they are working in a proper way or not."

Cankat Şimşek, friend (Lawyer)

"No matter whether you are a trial and error man or you are a kind of person who relies on designing every detail precisely before going to the development stage, testing is one of the most indispensable elements to have a robust or at least a 'sufficiently working' system. Having a solid testing team is the most reasonable and cheapest way of keeping the prestige of a producer."

Barış Pazarbaşı, friend (Business Analyst)

"Checking if a thing is broken or not."

The Cleaning Lady (Negative Tester)

"Checking if a thing is working or not."

The Doorkeeper (Positive Tester)

Note: *To tell the truth, these people are not randomly selected. They are the ones whom I see and chat with most often.*

INDEX

P

Performance testing, 70, 73
Platform, 2, 12, 75
Precondition, 74
Priority, 4, 18, 54, 75
Process-driven, 77-78
Proof of concept (PoC), 41-42, 74, 78

Q

Quality assurance (QA), 4, 6, 13, 15, 21, 39, 96

R

Random checking, 66-68
Regression testing, 25, 50, 53-54, 96
Release management, 73, 75
Requirement, 6, 12, 15, 17, 25, 35, 39, 42, 44, 60, 62, 70, 73-74, 90, 96, 98
Requirement coverage, 25
Risk management, 44
Root cause, 12, 25, 75, 85, 87, 94

S

Schedule, 25, 26-27, 37-38, 43,44
Script, 15, 31, 74-75, 89
Security, 48, 76, 95
Service level agreement (SLA), 36
Severity, 75
Shelfware, 42
Social weighting, 85
Software development, 2, 4, 9, 10, 12-13, 15, 21-22, 28, 39, 57, 94
Software development life cycle (SDLC), 15, 22
Software Usability Measurement Inventory (SUMI), 58
Static testing, 4, 44
System under test, 53

T

Test artifact, 74
Test automation, 47-48, 50-51, 53, 73-75, 84
Test case, 9-10, 13, 25, 41, 47-48, 51, 53-54, 61, 74-75, 81, 89, 96, 99

ABOUT THE AUTHOR

Barış Sarıalioğlu has over ten years of experience as an information systems professional. He is highly experienced in software development life cycle, project management, agile development, quality assurance, and software testing.

Barış also has diverse experiences spanning several industries, including telecommunications, defense, banking and finance, semiconductor manufacturing, and aviation. Based on this broad experience, he has been involved in several challenging projects and had the chance to work in several different countries, including Turkey, the United States, Russia, Germany, China, and Greece.

He has written articles and papers on software development methodologies, quality assurance, and software testing, and he regularly attends international and national conferences as a speaker, panelist, moderator, and contributor.

Currently, he is one of the managing partners of Keytorc Software Testing Services, where he holds the responsibilities of delivering test consultancy, outsourced test management, and software testing training.

www.ingramcontent.com/pod-product-compliance
Lightning Source LLC
LaVergne TN
LVHW052305060326
832902LV00021B/3721